Contents

III   OUT OF CHAOS

IV   SOME PEOPLE

Royal Festival Hall
on the South Bank

LIFE CYCLES

poems 1966–1996

M.A.B. Jones

BRENTHAM PRESS

First published 1996 by
Brentham Press, 40 Oswald Road, St Albans AL1 3AQ

ISBN 0 905772 51 2 15/2/97

British Library Cataloguing-in-Publication Data:
A catalogue record for this book is available from the British Library.

DTP by Gillian Durrant
Printed in England by Watkiss Studios Ltd, Biggleswade, Beds SG18 9ST

Acknowledgments

These poems have been published in a wide variety of magazines and anthologies, including: *Anglo-Welsh Review, Counterpoint, Country Life, Country Quest, Doors, Homes and Gardens, Iota, Orbis, Ore, Outposts, Poet's England, Poetry Nottingham, Poetry Wales, Reynard, Salopian Poetry, Success, Symphony, Ver Poets' Voices, Vision On* and *Weyfarers*.

Others have been broadcast and several have won awards, including first prize at Eisteddfodau in South Wales and Minsterley (Shropshire).

I THE YEAR TURNS

Rondeau: The Year

The year has turned after its winter blight
of rain and wind, of ice and frost and snow.
The chill air softens, harsh gales cease to blow,
days lengthen; we rejoice at early light.

The cherry clothes itself in clouds of white,
rivers and limping streams begin to flow;
The year has turned after its winter blight
of rain and wind, of ice and frost and snow.

Each opening leaf and flower brings fresh delight.
Drab fields and gardens now begin to show
the life that through dead months was hidden below.
Sweet Spring begins, darkness has taken flight.
The year has turned after its winter blight.

March Outlook

Barometer down, the day blusters,
clouds billowing like pillowslips
grey-white on a line.

Dry leaves cluster
in corners of the blown garden,
withering as cold winter
slowly warms to spring.

A spatter of drops blisters the window
and weather on the march
now crowds toward April.

Seville Oranges

Into a cold kitchen hazardous
with chill north wind stammering at glass
the outlook treacherous
they brought the colour of summer.
Great clouds heavy, yellow with threat of snow
paled before sight of them, rich, golden
sitting there piled in a blue plastic bowl.

Rough-textured the orange globes, glowing
centred the room, seemed like some
masterly still-life pictured
on cool grey walls. And the scent, the scent sweet
pervasive as fragrance of flowers
in warm greenhouse or southern
evergreen grove. As I entered
my mind turned from trouble, the crass world
in a turmoil, undone. And winter?
Winter was suddenly gone.

Making Marmalade

Of course there's an easy method –
machine or mincer. But satisfaction
lacks that way. Liking to use hands,
fingers bring delight to those with time.

Cutting-up is a slow process,
knife-risky. The blade jerks
stiffly on thick peel, can slant off,
damage hands. But once stripped,
slivers are quick to snip, a pleasure
to see piled in the bowl.

Aroma, romance come with slicing,
scent with the cut peel. You think of
dark groves glossy with leaf,
fragrant blossom, fruit slowly forming,
the green globe ripening,
yellowing in the hold of a ship.

Then back to practicalities –
a steady boil-up of peels,
addition of juicy flesh, stir of sugar
in the turmoil of cooking.

Testing for the set, the sure moment
when all is safely done, you wait
for a sense of achievement –
warm-up at the joyous sight
of clear jelly cooling
in the orange glass pots.

Spring

They have planted new trees for the old
where the crude brash red of the council brick
breaks like a rash into the cleared square.
The aged who seek new independence there
may watch the sapling strengthen, will not sit
in the shade of the grown tree or see
the shadow lengthen when sun extends it.
Their days will then be done.
                                    But Spring is theirs
now for the taking, the delicate shoots
unfolding, breaking.
These smooth young limes already tender,
bright polished buds with wine-dark shellac scales
and pale green leaves clustered on angled branches.
What man with half a hundred years to live
could hope to see a greater splendour?

Rondeau: the Rose

Rose, Queen of Flowers, so rich a prize,
sweet-scented joy we recognise
as glory of our summer morn -
shot-silk that yet thinks fit to warn,
that hides its sting in such disguise.

Your secret makes us realise
how life deceives and often lies.
But Rose, how wise to ring with thorn!
Oh Rose, how wise.

How clever you to tantalise,
set spines beside a lovely guise
of bud and blossom to adorn
our gardens every summer morn -
teach us life can be otherwise!
Oh Rose, how wise.

Midsummer Sonnet

Now are the hedges with bright garlands strown,
crowned with the pearl-cupped flower of the rose:
A cloth of gold, its bounty richly grown,
the eglantine its sweet profusion throws.
Knots of red campion star the lush green bank;
the trees in dark magnificence embower
a massed luxuriance of herbage rank,
laced with medallions of the elderflower.
    The road, blue-metalled in the hollowed deep
    curves to the sun and rises to the hill;
    the whole wide countryside now rests asleep,
    the birds in copse and meadow mute and still.
    The fields, the distant hills, the valleys lie
    in summer radiance open to the sky.

Shires in a Country Field

Marc's Red Horses could hardly frolic
more sportively than these. A moving frieze
variegate colours objectified
on screens of English-summer trees
they snuff free air after the crowd of towns.
Not as their forebears did, forcing swift pace
the battle once begun, but skittishly
frisking for joy, released from the trace
taut restriction of shaft, the drag of the dray.

Ripple of muscle flowing shoulder to rib
mane, fetlock flying, feathering the grass
of holiday pasture they sail rough seas
of wavy green, whinnying as they pass.
Stock-still at the fence we watch with frank amaze
town horses setting a country field ablaze.

Summer 1975

This is not any more the land we know.
The baked earth blenches, bleaches to near-white.
Nothing on dust or desert-waste can grow.

No breeze of early morning nor a slow
haze of the evening steals away the heat.
This is not any more the land we know.

There is no rain. No longer rivers flow
in spate or waterfall to bring delight.
Nothing on dust or desert-waste can grow.

Gardens burn russet-brown. No fork or hoe
will pierce the rock-hard soil. Colour takes flight.
This is not any more the land we know.

The early harvest droops. Hot sunset glow
swallows each day, invades each restless night.
Nothing on dust or desert-waste can grow.

The stunted pasture shrinks. Cattle, sheep show
by bellow, plaintive cry their fearful plight.
This is not any more the land we know.
Nothing on dust or desert-waste can grow.

Mirage

Swing-window tilted, I see in clear glass
a lake created where no water was.
I stand astounded as slow moments pass.

An underwater flora bottle-green,
a dappled mottled coppice darkly seen
swims in deep shadow with a surface sheen.

Beneath inverted trees black-pattern spaced
in neat flat silhouette on silver, laced
by frond and tendril fly-in-amber based

lie hidden mysteries. In crevice, crack
water-sprite, naiad lurk. There is no lack
of life in that lacustrine forest track.

Imagination as a winged bird flies
can find oases where no substance lies.
Dreams from ungrounded suppositions rise.

The window swinging back again to close
once more this torrid-summer garden shows
parched leaf, its only charm a fading rose.

The Moth

Blade-thin upon the lintel of the door,
seeming a scrap of dessicated leaf
blown by the wind against the paint, no more,
delicate, minute and frail beyond belief,
a golden moth with tiny wings outspread
lay in the sun. No ordinary eye
could see the fine antennae, each a thread
of fine-spun silk, lying enchantingly
in perfect curve. But, by glass magnified,
these and the marvellous filigree of lace
were visible, beauty intensified
by the feathered wing-edge - such amazing grace,
such intricate perfection of design
reflecting, in small compass, the divine.

Magpie

The predatory bird
perched on the topmost pole
of this whole neighbourhood
watches
and waits.

Altering stance,
angles round,
surveys the clustered trees
that make our small copse.

Ten minutes,
twenty,
he will sit until
some secret stir among leaves
betrays his prey.

Then,
poised for flight,
he swoops missile-like,
deadly dart to the swift kill.

Owl

Alighting feather-soft he made landfall
out of the sudden air just where we stood:
stayed seconds in summer dusk, surviving
close scrutiny. Finally,
a weighted puffball,
winged off in flight into his secret wood.

Quince

Native of central Asia
set at a whim in lawn
lying between house and park,
the quince bears first-time fruit.
Lemon-yellow globes
festive as Christmas lamps
glow in October inviting
reminiscence of past circumstance.

For one the large-scale garden
bearing hope of family future
never maturing. Another's
idyllic interval in small-time
existence, island
centring a busy millstream.
Fugitive blossom
climbing a brief summer.

Two separate dreams,
flame quickly dimmed only to grow
united in a winter
rosy as holly warming to the snow.

The Climbing Hydrangea

My last sight of it, late autumn,
small lemony leaves falling
in frost, piling up drifts
at the shrub's tortured roost.

This time of year the fence
bristles with bud - bright criss-cross
of sturdy mahogany twig
reaching out to the light.

Winter has turned it from drab
to warmth of rich russet-brown.
Soon tender green will feather
frenetic lattice-weave of the wood,

top-dress of delicate leaf
race across trellised length
of the supportive screen.
Then from the tight-furled bud
will flower perpetual spring

And Now November

Late Spring, coming with lushness
and flurry of blossom,
raced by, swift
as an April shower.
Then, with no time to watch
the slow progress of opening flower,
bud to uncurling petal,
we were rushed into full summer.

Blackthorn was there,
shining as a bride's white coronet.
Close-clustered pearls
rounded at morning, starred in warmth
of afternoon sun. Barbed twigs
And pinpoint leaves spread
pale stiletto shadow on springing grass.
The quickening hedge hid birds at nest.

Iris, spearheading the rest
purpled in green swords. Thrusting
from black earth, the whole of summer
laid carpeted colour. We were dazed,
amazed at the quick uprush, each day
a new surprise. But soon, too soon
the warm months passed to a glory
of radiant autumn, a threat of winter.

And now November cloaks the cherry
in a haze of thin rain, its last
few leaf-rags dangling in sad
dejection. The circling year
nears Christmas again. Holly reddens,
shops light with transitory brightness
to banish December dark
and gardens rest in a semblance of sleep.

Chrysanthemums for Christmas

The first crisp scent of them
signifies Autumn - Virginia Creeper
blazing on grey house-walls,
October fires spiralling
thin smoke into sunset skies
and gardens lush
with final flare of the late summer.

Long after dahlias
flash catherine wheels into bright whorls
and the last curled flush of roses
drops full-sculptured petals,
chrysanthemums linger.
Lighting up sombre days
they herald a wealth of Christmas pleasure,
bring New Year promise
of certain Spring.

Frost Flowers

In winter, blossoming in a cold night,
stars leaning to earth across a sky
brilliant with light, the frost-flowers come.
When morning breaks their crystal petals crowd
the inlaid window: where the plain glass was
white tendrils curl upon a jewelled stem.
By every radiant frond of every leaf
lie delicate whorls; each a perfected gem.

Brief beauty! See how the belated sun
climbing to warm the day dissolves
the spun-glass filigree. These scintillant flowers
this sparkling tracery of leaves make one
with beaded raindrops on the pane,
The blossoms, foliage, sheer delight all gone.

Dead End

Spring gives no promise yet - the Christmas rose
loses its whiteness. Aconites, paper-thin,
fade in chill air; the early snowdrops close.

There is no morning uprush of the mind.
Each day's slow apathy spins out the hour.
Rain drizzles down, sleet slants, the wind's unkind.

Late winter lingers now, though day's dim light
loiters before the dark. Turn up the fire
against the threatened cold of coming night.

Joy in the Morning

A sunlight shaft across the wall,
a shadow-flash lightly let fall
from a bird's wing - and all

the house throws off its winter gloom,
gaiety flooding every room.
So slight a thing, a bird's swift flight

and yet enough, mere shadow on a wall
to bring delight, illumine all.

II NO LAND SO RICH

Roots

Hut sites, streets stand out
defying time. Surviving war,
ravages of long weathering,
inroads of coulter, plough,
the confidential tales
deeply inscribed in soil
now yield to a candid glance
from the prying helicopter.

Probed by the keen camera's eye,
embedded surfaces reveal
secrets long kept by cropped cornfield
or rough upland pasture.
A Roman fort
complete with siege-camp,
town with forum, amphitheatre,
and springing to sight at times
surprisingly,
the planned projection
of a Celtic field-system.

Learning from the land
we find our roots fixed
in a firm context.
To match this
must needs build with equal insight.

Village

None sees the pageant whole.
Yet its long history lies
in these limited acres
limned here on a map.
A few plough teams,
areas of harsh meadow held of Norman lords
and all shared by a handful of freemen.
This was its listing at Domesday.

Scant rainfall,
same soil stiff to plough,
a bitten climate,
wind whipping in from the east
still meet its people. How the rest has changed!

Strangers born in far towns
live in the midst. Where once
some thirty reapers took the field,
sang as they went, scythed the ripe corn
with blades lustrous as silk,
a single figure now
high on a tractor sweeps the harvest in.

Between the then and now
the unknown under churchyard grass,
those with brief fame
immortalised on stone or the walled brass.
And deeper still in loam
remnants of older people, older ways,
fabric of Rome, the broken shards
of yet more ancient days.
In these few acres lie
all legend, history. Homes, customs change.
Only the land, immutable
sees the swift centuries pass.

Country Church

Out of the summer sun
into this ancient church,
Step from this modern world
back into distant time.
Drop for a moment's space
the noise and the outward din
Let the peace of the cold chill stone
enter within.

Gaze at the Norman font
Finger its sculptured skill
Marvel the minds that wrought
here on an ancient hill
treasure on treasure stored
this building of Cotswold grey
Think of the golden glint of stone
on the first day.

See in the pillar round
strength that the mason set.
Eight hundred years have gone
Eight hundred years and yet
still soars its massive might
Still its magnificent height
tells of the man's deep faith and speaks
of his sure Heaven.

Out of the summer sun
Turn for a moment's space
into this ancient church -
Accept its grace.

Cotswold Village

See how the underlying stone
dictates this landscape! Manor, cottage, barn
the ancient church, the very flower and tree
are all determined by its quality.
Here in the village where the mason wrote
an austere manuscript, chiselled and shaped
with practised skill each slice of quarry-face,
mark well his masterpiece.
Watch light when sun resumes dominion lift
the modulated grey to lambent gold.
See brightness fall on doorway, dripstone,
mullion, architrave. Each opulent part
of this conjoint and close-knit harmony
reciprocates, when vagrant sunbeams play,
the luminous mood of a resplendent day.

Barns

Their high gables rising
above lofty aisles,
massive roof-trees seen dimly from below
give them an aloof majesty
as of some fine cathedral.... Built-to-last
floors of oak, local stone-brash or gravel
beaten into place until the rock-hard
surface rang like metal,
they offered room, leisure
- harvesting over - to take ease.
Cleared for feasting, grain safely housed,
their huge proportions,
great space designed for the flail's use,
furnished a setting grand enough
for ceremonial, gracious for dance.
Once a dozen wagons waited,
stacks piled inside. Now the vast doors
hang wide, chill strikes, an emptiness
echoes from blank walls.... But, walking
outside where sun climbs the square buttresses
supporting these stories in stone,
cold has gone. Here, in broad fields, warm, golden,
strong temples of a corn-goddess stand,
ripe with years, perpetually young.

English County

Sussex has seen it all - the upward climb
surveying history's expanse of time.

Hill-villages above a trackless Weald
Channel both hazard and a hoped-for shield.

Flintmines and settlements, low tumuli
earthworks on sites to scan the land and sea.

A changing scenery, bare upland Down
clothed with the Roman beech, a windtossed crown.

Saxons to pioneer the forest ways
build huts of timber, wattle and to raise

primitive churches - Sompting's Rhenish tower
Normans to conquer in their finest hour.

Sussex has known them all and later still
watched as the summer gorse bearded each hill

menacing shadows like great vultures fly
threatening invasion from a wartime sky.

Yet now survives, living epitome
as counties are of England's history.

Meditation at Hampton Court

Levelled by centuries, the smooth lawns spread
beyond my window.... sitting here at ease,
needle in hand, repairing tapestries
with cautious skill, I think of all the dead

who walked these passages and rooms outspread
throughout this ancient house: Wolsey, who planned
increasing range of buildings to expand
his fame - then fending fall from favour, fled

presenting it to Henry: Kings and queens
who flourished, faded in these gracious halls -
some locked in intrigue, clothed in secret walls,
for better fortune paying go-betweens.

And one, like Jane in her historic past,
tense with the fear that, hidden within her womb
a girl child grew, one that would spell her doom,
leave her neglected, torn from grace, outcast.

Maid to two queens before, putative maid
to Henry - what smooth analgesic thought
soothed quick betrothal, speedy marriage, brought
peace to a troubled heart, disturbed mind, swayed

by London crowds who murmured at a king
(so fickle in his loves, so wayward, hard),
who watched with dark distrust, no pity barred,
the cruel block at Anne's dismembering.

What monstrous fate! To bear a son, ensure
continued favour: sense that future fade
in days of dim remembering, hopes betrayed
by life's delusion, see death at the door!

I take my needle up.... Did this worn weave
darken the window where she lay in pain?
I shiver - turn my mind to work again,
blench at the thought that life can so deceive.

Essex

I remember it,

myself, raw, brash, just beginning
life in a strange setting.
How I missed the hills! Born between
Cotswold, Malvern, seeing always
a tumbled skyline, I was too exposed,
too vulnerable under those open skies.
But soon the Essex charm
working small miracles possessed me –
pargetting, a weatherboarded house,
the frequent watersplash. Later,
surprised, I saw the splendid tapestry
of cloud move over Constable landscape,
dramatic broad wheatland with larks
rising into spirals of song.

Looking back, three jewels beautifully
set: Thaxted with Morris dancers in the street;
Maldon, three-quarters sky, the rest
thin masts and spars on a blue day,
creeks dotted with boats keeled over.
And quince in Spring, pink-candy buds
enamelling a quick-green hedge
at the Mill House towering over a shallow stream.

Journey into Norfolk

A late Spring breaking
into oakleaf bronze, downdroop
of folded chestnut meeting us
en route, and Norwich
a spread of shadowy trees
on blue roads, small shallow valleys
full of willow, tiny rivers.

Countryside huge with sky,
wide spaces, freshness of washed flint
keeping age at bay. Great churches
sailing shiplike on a green ocean,
the plain landscape lacking hedges –
a haze of fields, vast cornbelts.

Yarmouth out of season a sandy waste
recalling David, an upturned
superannuated boat and little Em'ly
on a stretch of beach
looking out to a treacherous sea.

Bristol, I Love You

How could I fail to fall for you,
seeing you first in a thin rain
of autumn leaf falling on prim
Victoria, stolid on her plinth
in College Green - trams rollicking round
a Centre still harbouring ships, and the sky
bright with promise of my new student-world.

Later, when rapier searchlights
lit your face of gaping holes,
your great gutted churches gateways
to havoc - when I picked my way
across glass, stones, a crisscross
of hosepipes at morning - I knew,
Bristol, your courage would hold me.

Your war-scarred winter gripped me
more than brave autumn or sweet spring,
when Downs were a hawthorn-mist
and gardens a glory of lilac, laburnum.
Forged in war's fire, Love's ligature's
loosed by no time-corrosive year.

Bristol

In May laburnum
Lilac draped grey walls, the Downs
were hawthorn-haze. When young
life in the city built on hills
was heaven. Spring in those bright
perfervid days heady perfume,
Summer eternal dream.

Later the steady drone,
dark symphony of planes. Winter
saw streets laid waste, carpets
of debris, splintered glass. Black flakes,
malignant snow fell on a town
exposed to pitiless gods,
Men in a red-hot holocaust
fighting impossible odds.

The city stared today, stranger
where bombs rained down. I walked new ways,
old ways transformed, all changed
in brilliant sun. Walked in uneasy peace
lost in a dream under skies
where once the thunder of guns hung low
and stark white searchlights stalked.

No Land So Rich

No land so rich
in rivers latticed with the white stars
of water-crowfoot, nymphs, larvae,
ephemera, small shrimps flicking on stems.
After winter the water clearing
you stare at stones, shillets in the stream
creating a stippled tapestry of flecks, freckles.
Ribbons of bright green begin to shimmer.
Summer nears.

Each spring the miracle. White roots
seek sun from an iced clarity
of crystal water-run, put forth tendrils
to ripple, wave with wild abandon.
Soon the milky way extends, hazes
to the next bend, caddis in houses
of stick, speck, hiding under slabs.
Trout lurk. No land so rich
in rivers, streams dappled,
mazed with mysteries of a million stars.

River Town
Shrewsbury

Day's colour now withdrawn, the painted sky
hangs backcloth to the town - each tapering spire,
bold parapet, square tower cut-silhouette,
precise black-patterned templet, shade thrown down
in crazy ripple to the river's reach.
Uneasy, weak, quivering reflections lap
at tethered boats, at wrack that rides the flood.
This twilight hour sees the whole city drown.
Soon a full thousand lamps illuminate
the theatre of night, small moons strung out
pendent in space, resplendent bauble hung
high over streets that climb the lighted hill.
Below, now rising from its darkened grave
the sunken city shines beneath the wave.

Severn Elvers

The Severn scoops them up,
sucks in its gaping mouth
a shoal of grey transparencies.

Travellers through secret seas,
Atlantic's undertow
the dense mass swiftly moves upstream.

Fine food for pike, perch, bream,
the heron's heavy glut –
an early Easter harvest-cull

upriver after full
of tide. Broad ribbons run,
contour the curving bank, are caught

by torchlight, netted taut.
A foaming, squirming catch
in former times street-cried

in towns on Severnside.

Church in Apedale

Travelling in summer
the long divisive ridge, crest of a wave
piled high, ready to break over
the broad fertile plain, you stumble upon it
at the hot dead end of a road
that narrows down to a mere ribbon-strip.
Placed here, emphatic stop, the village clings
- small dot on a scaled ordnance map -
about its Norman church.

Beneath rich overhang of woods
spilling from Wenlock Edge, the squat tower stands
cool sanctuary under the hill. Threading
an ancient gate that creaks its rusty hinge,
you pass blunt square-cut pillars, climb
through coarse and untrimmed grass
where purple scabious lifts a tufted head.

Within, an ornate font. Some craftsman's skill,
following tradition, must have carpentered
its tall and tapered top. Walking
his forebear's steps, he must have strolled
out from his workshop to the fields around,
found inspiration there. Carving
a stylised stook of corn, he fashioned it
with simple joy .... Fingering the grain,
I pay my silent tribute to the man
who shaped with artless flair
and in his Maker's praise,
these stiff stalks grooved like fluted corduroy.

March Journey

But for the jumbled hills crowding around,
red soil running south, you could have said
Cuyp making his picture-magic of some
Dutch landscape. There was no haze -
the day light, bright as the heart of summer.
Cattle stood freckled, statuesque
on flat pastures, grazed Welsh Borderland
in stock attitudes of painted ease.

From the train, not a ruin in sight.
The March, once moated, fortified,
lay to the west.... Hard, on that day -
young winter corn drilling peaceable fields,
a plough sailing brown seas in a cloud of dust -
to credit the turbulent past. No sign
of earthwork mound, square keep, the scene
imperturbable, staid. Those age-old
skirmishes buried deep.

And as, unheard through glass, a dizzy lark
fluttered its spiral into the high unseen,
the diesel, speeding past farmyards, trees,
reaped a first harvest
of green after green.

The Dam: Clweddog

Striding the dominant height
above valleys where lush hedgerows
quicken with running green
and paintbrush poplars sweep
to a sky washed clean by spring rain,
the great white arches of the dam
straddle the wide gully. This cicatrice
scarring the landscape steps slowly down,
trickles the gathered waters from the lake
hid in the bowl of hills. Tall buttresses
frown on battalions of militant larch
rounding the lower slopes: paths hang
precipitous on the sheer sharp edge
of deep ravines, cling resolute
to fearful escarpments and mount
with the springing turf to the summit.

The patched worn skin of earth is stretched
over these high hills. Leonine
they lie crowning the countryside,
tawny under bright fitful sun,
dark-dappled beneath racing clouds,
guarding the man-made marvel.
A solitary buzzard circles the keen air.

Seashore

Sea-fret and feathers of foam
pattern soft wet sand.
At this near–distance
indigo and violet stiffen
green folds of ocean
whence snow-white rollers
fling flocked jetsam on the beach.
Olive-brown bladderwrack
festoons collections
of clean smooth shells, puffs yellow
balloons on broad straps
strung out among bleached cuttlefish blades.

Scanning the damp marbled floor
children seek treasures,
bare foot clenching the ridged edge
of a ribbed and pebbled shore.
Out here on the waterline
this flaccid jellyfish,
seeming some vast paperweight
tossed far by turbulent wave,
displays its purple flower
embedded deep in the glaze.
Glistening in hot sun
it placidly waits
the evening incoming tide.

Escape

Impatient to see it you climb
the last steady headland.
A slow pull hauls up the rise,
green earth folding behind. There
before you an incandescent sea,
spread of brisk sparkling wave,
heady air sweeping in
as a swift tide-drift.

Peace speaks in white foamflecks
feathering the blue surface,
writes its placid message
on rippled sandribs. Below bents,
tussocks of rough marram,
brown seawrack edges,
the curved straggle of bitten shore.
No distraction. You are here alone.

Time, space to know yourself.
No voices, noise. But the bleak
cry of gulls, rising bustle of wind
dissolves intoxication,
brings taste of salt,
bitter storm battering at ships
your own frail barque
back in the knock of waves, rages,
dark gulf of life, the roaring sea.

Carnac
(Les Alignements du Menec)

A chequered blue
roofing the flat expanse of land
spills sun and shadow equally.

Do not confuse
glacial erratics, natural stacks
among earth's standing stones with these.

These which stand free
in long alignments narrowing
to mists of lost antiquity.

Which wait upon
a later comprehending mind
a future brain computer-kind,

some chip or flake
to probe man's dim religious past
with silent proton light to make

their sacred plan
a purpose clear to those who knew
the helplessness of early man

plain to his heirs.
Standing today among these stones
we sense the power they felt at dawn

touch at the hem
of seamless garments worn in faith
woven by gods for simple men.

Geysir
(Iceland)

Suddenly provoked, the blue eye,
salt-encrusted, spouts a tall jet
shoots into thin air. Tantalised
photographers crouching to get
their best shot yet jerk with surprise.
Hearing their agitated cries

the rest of us flock to the spot,
watch for the next tinged aperture
to spurt. The ground around us quakes
or so we think when told that future
years will see land break away
drift to Shetland, Greenland over grey

Atlantic wave. This blistered knot
of cratered pockmarks crowds the earthbound space
much as the moon's holed surface seen
through probing telescope. An awesome place?
Cheerful expectancy ferried us here
but fancied instability
now brings us to the nearer edge of fear.

Norway

Last time, nineteen-thirty-six
there were rain-storms. Sun too at intervals
glinting prismatic falls,
the same painters' paradise.
But knives, half-poised to strike
were sharpening in Europe,
preparing for the holocaust.

Young then, politically aware
the whole land seemed remote,
not to belong to troubled consciences.
People of myth not mystery,
no complication, a country
scarce worth the conquering. Who would want
those steeps, deeps, volcanic outcrops?

Now I have seen
in the soft clarity of light, shadows
of violent street-fighting, cliffs defying
more than the ocean like a clenched fist.
Small towns, conspicuous churches rise cleanly,
monumental over their dead,
the deeps hide treachery
and Quisling remains a name for traitors.

On Receiving a Copy of Baedeker's *Rheinlande*, 1931

Ulrich whose book this was, Officer,
Secret Resister aiding hunted

Jews holed up underground and hiding
wanted children, German Aryan

refugees could call friend, I salute
you over a gap of thirty years.

The package, centenary Baedeker
arrived recorded mail to set me

wondering (not birthday or Christmas).
Surprise stopped with the letter unwrapped

but at your story thus come to light
I was caught in a wash of sick grief.

War nearly over, why grow careless
leave name-lists in a barrack locker

get locked up - was it subconscious wish
to end a too-complex existence

desire to take what retribution
might be due? If so, it came quickly.

Americans nearing, your Nazi
wardens jibbing at political

prisoners panicked, hastily shot.
Ulrich, the book rich in maps, coverage

of a countryside lying to hand
guides me, leads me back to more, much more

than your loved and what you felt to be
reprobate and desecrated land.

III   OUT OF CHAOS

Beginnings

In the beginning....
was it dark
just formless, void?

The questions start.
What brought
that morning fireball
riding high –
moon god haunting
the night vault
of a pinpricked sky –

flints knocked to shape
fossils or figured stones
striated build of rock.
Lightning, the shock
when ground trembled
and the crazy earth shook.

Let's praise observers
noting trivial things:
odd shells, ice, minerals
the flow of rivers, flowers:
explorers, theorists who saw
openings to other worlds than ours.

Mathematicians,
scientists
probing galaxies of suns,
moon, Milky Way,
limits of space and sound,
all those who actively
seek in hope to find
small vestige of beginning
or prospect of an end.

Genesis

The main tales stick. All early history -
Heaven, Earth created; Day, Night, Sun and Star:
Man made from dust; Serpent, the evil scar
on life; eventual delivery
of Israel's children to the Promised Land.
The Book tells all, but youthful minds demand
a right to question. Science opens doors,
casts doubt on old beliefs, ascertains fact,
discards tradition in the very act.
But, as it seeks for Truth, fresh knowledge pours.
All speaks of Order, of a Mind that planned,
slowly revealing with a Master-hand.

Man on the Moon

Setting foot there, first human to view
its pockmarked blank desolation
he took its measure as the pristine moon
worshipped by primitives, same face
turned always toward earth,
had timelong measured man.

Stark black shadows, blind-white surface
stared, outfaced him. Yet
that unmatched moment must be met.
No roving camera's eye
listing scarred violence or the charcoal rock
powdered to dust could register
the mind's immensity, its sense of joy.

Time whistling by, the scientist
took charge. Exhilaration passed.
Elation giving way to ordered care
in completion of mundane tasks,
Man's giant leap into the great unknown
shrank to one small cautious step.

Monuments

Eager
to keep green
memories of past achievement,
We set them petrified
on plinths in parks,
great squares, public gardens.
Rain, wind, long years
of aftermath wash over them, hard ones
weathering storms successfully,
remaining as in life impressive.

Others of softer mettle wear away,
seem weatherbeaten, impotent
to meet the winds of change,
live under a cloud. As a child
seeing one such I asked innocently
who was he, why has he lost face?

Carving in stone
blank-eyeballed images of men
an odd but human trait.
Standing alone, exposed
above the crowd, they seem
to seek the empty void, symbolise
our own rooted desire to rise.
Putting them there
some recognition of our solitary state,
our own purblinded eyes.

Fame is the Spur
(Murchison 1792-1871)

I like to think of him
bowling along Shropshire roads
in a smart phaeton,
countryfolk wondering
at the huge wave of Wenlock Edge
fringed with his two spanking greys
outlined on the skyline.

Striding hillsides, tapping rock
to ascertain origins of the Earth's crust
some need to expend energy
left from foreign campaigns
drove him on. Or was it an urge
for fame, forages in Sicily, Portugal
fading before the thrill
of finding fragments, fossils
to encapsulate memory
in the world's annals?

In the end it was Wales
that captured the name. Doubling back
Brecon to Builth he found the missing link
in low ridges, grey rock sinking,
rising again under Old Red Sandstone.
Calling it Silurian he gave Salop
through Ludlow and Wenlock beds
a final grand salute.

Menai Suspension Bridge
(Telford)

You cannot see it without sensing
the man's character; those huge stanchions
striding the land giant-like
Holds built irretrievably into rock
The superstructure airy, flexible.

Telford, architect, engineer
of a hundred roads, canals, aqueducts
identified by his work. Neither luck
nor the strength, elegance of the finished bridge
should hide his dedicated toil
or blind us to the size of his consummate task.

On the far side Mona. Throwing a road
across that tricky strait startling enough.
Aerial way, rock to rock, quixotic dream.
But nothing conquered him. After
opening of quarries, construction of quays
Seven arches taking four years to build,
the two main piers. Think of them
a hundred and fifty-three feet high,
Every stone closely scrutinised
by a past-master of his art.

And the sixteen vast chains, thirty-six bars
to each tested in his Shrewsbury workshop,
Welded together, braced with iron wire.

What a day to watch from the shore!
Ends fixed immovably, a loaded raft
towed to midstream before high tide and Telford
himself giving the hoistaway.
How the fife-band played, the boisterous crowd
cheering men turning those Anglesey capstans
lifting the great centre-piece.

Spanning the gap a monument
to faith and work. As darkness fell,
the night sky ravaged by flare after flare
and the whole coast signalling beacon-fire,
Thomas, intent on what was yet to come
recluse in his room at prayer.

Clifton Suspension Bridge
(Brunel)

The Sea Walls view
distanced by haze supposes
cobwebs afloat, a filigree,
a slender necklace strung
on river-throat.
Its robust strength
crossing between colossal towers
surprises. Chains triple-tiered,
girders, links, rods
speak with such purpose
hung from rooted piers.

Brunel's 'first darling child',
final memorial. Sketching the sky
with aerial grace,
the artist-engineer
writes with assertive flash
his personal signature –
writes it with verve, panache.

Darwin

Fearing abuse
he marshalled evidence
checked notes, experimented
through twenty cautionary years
before finally writing.
Mild, unprovocative
calm language reasoned theory
with defensive charm.

Months later the bombshell –
a bishop's rhetoric, jest,
spark of attack.
At home on invalid couch
bewildered, shocked
at statements never made
he heard it reverberate.

Recovering, stuck to his guns
knowing explosive truth
must erupt in earthquake.

Still Life
(Zurburan)

Against a backcloth
of intense black velvet,
orange-yellow globes
rise like tropic moons
on an orient night-sky
or goldglint of winter stars
splintered in northern climes.

I picture it
hung on some Spanish wall
of dark Cordovan leather.
Light gleams
striking from the left on metal
a shapely pot, matt fruit
a rose, the plaited coils
of a woven basket.

Zurburan's masterpiece
still-life, a kind of altar
clearing the mind
of clutter, restlessness
imposing order, peace.

The Loving Couple
(Rembrandt)

Drawn first by colour, texture, you approach
the red-gold glamorous. Who can they be?
But, near, the question of identity
fades before fear of guilt, that you encroach
on an occasion purely personal.
Arms, fingers, hands entwined so tenderly
such innocent young love asks privacy
an attitude almost devotional.
The worked and worried paint, the background-dark
throws up the yellow-red with power and force
light-shade as always proving Rembrandt's source
of two worlds linked, his never-failing mark.
Jewels and gestures, looks and vestments lent
for celebration of a Sacrament.

Vermeer

Colour he took, balanced design
as problems to be solved. He worked
at modest versions of his world –

still-life precision in those Dutch
interiors, views of Delft, small streets,
an Artist distanced in his studio.

Silence commands each scene with light
near-tangible, now brilliant, sharp,
now dimmed to a soft radiance

suffusing truth, intensifying
colour on a roof, on water,
folds of cloth, a door, wall, dress.

Himself always withdrawn, you feel
integrity, pay tribute to
an eye that looks into infinity.

Impressionist
(Monet)

Put distance between you and the picture.
Uncouth shapes crystallise, meaningless blobs
spell out sense. In 'Gare St. Lazare'
an engine motif emerges through mist.
No people to meet, part, but light
streams through glass, the artist
revealing its sequel in steam.

Creating his Argenteuil garden
studying vague fugitive forms
in water monopolised many years
sea providing the greatest challenge.

Transient cloud, ruffle of wind
stirring surfaces left small leisure
to mix, match colour. Swift strokes
gave rise to the critics' derisive use
of his own tentative title.

To see with childlike insight,
pin down sensation, keep watch
on sun, shadow, and paint outdoor
on the spot became primary aims.

Not a painting machine, he said,
to show finish. I reflect fleeting moments.
Nature never stands still.

Turner

A short man, hook-nosed
in an ill-cut coat, frilled shirt;
Chameleon, not without kindness.
There was affection for father, others.
But nothing human ever interfered
with his real love, the world of men
chiefly a place to escape from.
An artist-soul but a driver of hard bargains.

Minimal schooling, illiterate
yet worked unceasingly
no toil too severe. Sketched everything,
never spared effort. Once sailed
in a tempest lashed to the mast
to study the gale's uproar.

Nature and history
used to suit his great conceptions -
Hazes of light, mist, moisture.
Prismatic moods of lyrical elation,
Nocturnes in opal, amethyst,
And the later water-colours a dazzle
flashing in farragoes of bright glory.

Turner's Thames

Travelling today
by a cool Thames
the sight of yellow leaves
lit in late autumn
recalled his luminous touch.
The slender birch
waving feathery plume,
confetti coin flickering
gold in a light breeze,
the scene diffused and soft
as his tender brush.

If with such confidence
I could paint trees
as these early Turners
basking in afternoon sun,
I should shout my jubilation
from tall housetops,
could forget failure
ask none for reassurance,
need no consolation.

Model

Not sumptuously bedded
on ice-white linen or ivory silk,
but seated on a rough dais -
the students eye, appraise her;
earnestly try to transpose
arms, thighs, the curved beauty
of her breast to paper.

Here, shapeliness is all - she need not fear
Matisse's harsh distortion,
the sheer daring of a Blue Nude,
herself reduced to acute angles,
a body trading grace for power.

Unconscious of descent
in a long succession,
she knows little of Renoir, Cézanne,
still less of those painters
risking censure, imprisonment -
Goya under Inquisition
for the naked Maja,
Manet shocked at reaction
to Olympia, the public brandishing
umbrellas, sticks
at a modern version of Titian.

After exhausting sessions
she rests at ease, feet loosely slipped
into red mules, her gown
closely folded about her.
Conscious of need to gain
a bare living, she rejoices
in this brief interlude;
would prolong the luxury
of hot coffee, body-freedom
from the stiff, restricted placing
of the sitting.

Street Organ
(Amsterdam)

Into the Kalverstraat loud music pours
kindling the passion of a warmer day.
The town's cold humour colours up from grey
of sky to rose. The vibrant traffic roars.
With sudden energy one of the crowd
taps a tattoo with jaunty feet. Sound grows
vivacious, liquifies. Sheer fountain flows
in swift roulades, cascades. Before it, cowed
into submission by exuberance,
musicians' thought of balance and restraint,
fuss about tempo justo, nuance, glow faint
vanish in such superb self-confidence.
An organ jangling with rococo beat
transforms an hour, a mood, a city street.

Fantasia
(Beethoven Op. 27)

House shuttered, lucid in full sun
sonata in itself. Façade fronting
the Bonngasse preludes grace
of eighteenth-century elegance
curved iron-wrought stair mounting
to an upper space where he was born.

Seen from this open door the window
floods blank attic-loft with long light-shaft.
Moonlight must wash these walls,
fall with soft luminous sheen
upon the marble bust. Imagined
music filters from a far room.

His four-stringed last klavier rings out
in thin high tone the triune symmetry
of Opus Twenty-seven. Theme in strict form,
melody embellished, modified,
pure poem hides insidious load
of sorrow. Stunned by secret grief

deafness creeping thief-in-the-night,
Beethoven plays. Trees, forests, fields he loved
flower in the mind. Feeling, fire flow
from disciplined fingers, inert air grows
impetuous-swift to closing phrase until
sound faltering fails and the rapt fantasy

as quickly fades.

Ballerina

The corps de ballet waits. She takes the stage,
beauty assumed at will. Her great strength veiled,
becomes some fragile thing of unknown age -
a ghost - a phantom ship to harbour sailed.
Intangible, floats on an unseen sea,
is borne on wings, belongs to airy space;
music interpreted by poetry
leaving of worldly resonance no trace.

With heaven-bound elegance this art of dance
defies all natural law, soars to a height
of lyrical enchantment and will lance
through bonds that clinch too close to earth's dim sight.
All who delight in its elysium know
perpetual joy though dancers come and go.

Patineur

Mastery creates on this blurred
surface natural fantasy.
Body a bird in flight

scissoring with purposive wings,
his pinioned positioning
perpetual delight, he skims

swallow across an evening sky.
Crouched low, wings pleated, soon becomes
swan lighting on a reed-trimmed lake.

Slow-motion argosy for seas
limpid beneath a southern moon
he sails to day's calm windless close.

Illusion ending, spins
in dizzy circles curled into
the folded petals of a rose.

Conductor

Imposing silence, he demands
our whole attention. Orchestra,
singers alert, raises his hand,
signals the start of a great work.
Accepting direction, the choir rises as one.

From my near seat, I watch
each studied movement. A shrewd eye
sweeps his kingdom, all at command.
The small baton lifts - a slight nod -
and music swells, fills spaces, climbs
heights, walls to the far roof.

Hands move in unison.
There is grace, delicacy
in light touches, deft articulation
of curved fingers. Guiding
tenor, soprano, bass
he leads through intricate phases

of this sublime Mass.
Swaying on his low stand,
controlling rising tides
of flowing sound, he demonstrates
consummate power.
Glories in this, his finest hour.

Skills
(A Sicilian Quintet)

Where have they gone, the skills of yesterday –
the art informing all our early verse;
the easy flow of ballads apt to stay
in minds to learning otherwise averse.
Where have they gone, the skills of yesterday?

The high poetic craft with rhythm, rhyme,
alliteration of a Saxon Age,
Chaucer's shrewd, subtle voice, Milton's sublime
and lofty tone that leapt out from the page –
the high poetic craft with rhythm, rhyme?

I search the booklets, noting with dismay
a lack of Dryden's taut and compact line,
the gentle, natural pathos of a Gray.
Reluctant to relinquish such a sign
I search the booklets, note it with dismay.

The clumsy phrasing, lack of rhythmic time
marking our modern verse are plain to see.
Failing to get word, line and sense to chime,
how can we hope to gain felicity
by clumsy phrasing, lack of rhythmic time?

I look in vain for skills of yesterday.
Recalling all the art, the magic flow
of lyric poets who with classic play
of rhyme and rhythm charmed us long ago,
I look in vain for skills of yesterday.

Where have they gone, the skills of yesterday,
the high poetic craft with rhythm, rhyme?
I search the booklets, noting with dismay
the clumsy phrasing, lack of rhythmic time,
and look in vain for skills of yesterday.

The Quest

Collecting pebbles, shells
from strand and cove,
we start the early search
for treasure-trove.

Salvaged from ocean wrack
starfish, cuttlefish bone,
picked up at the tide's slack
with fluted limpet-cone

begin our lifelong craze
for what's our own.
The objects may amaze,
raise puzzled frown

in some who do not share
our dedication, zest.
But we who deeply care,
convinced our choice is best

can laugh aloud at those
whose different gem
will never prove our rose,
our diadem.

Yet all pursue the quest
for Love's sweet nonpareil.
Without relief or rest
this never-ending trail.

Go to the Ant....

Consider her ways, her history
far-reaching to Antiquity -
her multiple variety.

Her homes - in jungle, burning sand,
perpetual snow and every land
from Northern ice to coral strand.

Nomad, forever doomed to trace
a way through every earthly place
known - unknown - to human race.

Possessing power to build, create
cities with skill and cultivate
gardens in trees - and excavate.

Ants - which can form community,
will share a common destiny -
together work in unity.

Yet savagely will scour for food,
fight wars, to others bode no good,
an army bent on battle-mood.

Go to the Ant - but recognise
this is not wisdom: to be wise
needs more than instinct. Our true prize

is conscious thought, the gift of Mind
to plan, to form, to seek, to find
a better way for all Mankind.

IV SOME PEOPLE

Parezanin Speaks
(28.6.1914-28.6.1974)

Crossing the frontier - no passport - I
was picked up by guards, Gavrilo's
card tucked three prison days in my shoe.
The message memorised as promised
stayed with me, enigma unravelled
try as I would. But the Sarajevo man
who welcomed me smiled. He understood.

Back in the village black flags hung
from the mast. My sister, visiting
whispered of shots, the Archduke's death,
a man from Grahovo's sudden arrest.
Uneasy, holding my breath, my mind flew
quick as a gunflash
to our parting by turbulent Sava,
Gavrilo's request.

What followed? Father, grandfather hanged:
grandmother, hearing the news, choosing
to die by her own gentle hand.
The rest of us questioned and sentenced.
How could we guess, youngsters just wanting
our country free, what was to come -
teenagers hurrying with a gun
too ignorant to know the complicated web
of politics, the turn of fate, too blind
to visualise the loosened flood of hate.
From that ill-omened note who could foretell
Gavrilo, patriot, dying
scapegoat in his prison cell.

Ballad of the Pioneers
(USA 1776-1976)

Where cars today in a countless stream
run on the six-lane Interstate
the miners tramped, followed a dream
checked on the miles and carried the freight.

A rifle, an axe, and a bag of corn
good horse, good wife, salt, luck, good health
made for the feeling you'd been born
to venture West and capture wealth.

Cumberland Gap, Wilderness Road,
shades of Walker and Daniel Boone:
hitting the trail, no fixed abode
bed down later rather than soon.

Over the mountains, on and on
deep in the river, across the plain
assaulted by wind, burnt by the sun
deceived by bog, drenched by the rain.

Theirs was a journey none could desire,
rolling desert and rocky defile
a hundred and ten, the air on fire,
catsclaw, mesquite. The tempers rile.

But gold, gold, gold at the end of the trail.
Shake off the lumber, forsake the dead.
Once you're there you can hardly fail
to barter the metal for more than bread.

A few had luck - and muscle and guile
but Brandy Gulch and Poverty Hill
tell the sad tale of the many who fell,
those whom adventure managed to kill.

And the real pioneers were people who swarmed
clung to the land, planted and slaved,
created community, settled and farmed
eked out a living, half-starved and survived.

Trial, 1805
(Presteigne, Radnor)

Churchyard inscription tidily set out
purports to tell the tale. Infanticide.
Young, seventeen - the stone says beautiful,
implies regret that one so well-disposed
remained so long immune
to a right sense of Christian principle.
Wondering, we try to visualise the scene,
imagine what she felt facing
panoply of court, the solemn jurymen.
Could there be distraught hope
of mercy from a hanging judge?
Or was her mind, attuned to misery
bread, water, straw within the common jail,
already numbed?

Burdened by memory of her murdered babe
brief lover lost, too tired to contemplate
doctrinal truths, who in those last few days
was least at ease?
Awaiting execution the girl, shocked, dazed?
Or the Lord Justice Harding - no reprieve -
who sought to reconcile, to justify
verdict with reason to a child untaught.

Epitaph for Heloise

I lie beside him, where I longed to be
in life. After the scandalous days, his rape
at hands of hired assassins secretly
creeping by night, I feared the frightful shape
of time-to-come. The crucifying loss
of Astrolabe, our son, hardly came near
the searing of that desolating cross
I bore in my despair, year following year.

Waiting in vain for sight of him, a word
to ease the parting, growing old
held over me a Damoclean sword
chilling the spirit with impending cold.

In life divided, true to my last breath,
united now in hope of Heaven, through death.

Charlotte at Haworth

This warm autumnal day
crowds up the small open doorway.
Richmond's drawing
hangs on a patterned wall
bookcases fill fireside recesses
a lamp stands on a square table
polished to perfection.
We look in awe
at parlour-dining room,
safe fortress, longed-for home to those
banished to grieve in alien places.

This too the scene
of childhood fantasies, late evening dreams.
Here Thackeray
her Titan-genius hung
in gilded frame to cheer, uplift
at some rare time when life shone bright.
Here sister Emily
defended to the last her right to die.

All haunt the room
but Charlotte most.
The sun, fitful as ever, fades.
For five late years 'entombed' said one
she sat alone. Outside
frigid with latent rain the wild
November wind howled winter discontent
in barren garden-ground.
So many gone
herself left solitary there
to write, remember, mourn.

Exquisite Sister*

"More than half a poet", she said,
close-knit with William. In his work
her phrases shine - that stunted thorn,
the moon among a black-blue vault,
a whirl-blast from behind the hill,
the tossing, reeling daffodil,
a butterfly, the beggar seen in May.

Recording all, the walks, the Lakeland scene,
the talks, she sees herself
guardian, provider of a frame
to nurture genius. The homely images
slip from her pen - William sleeps well,
slept badly; William sat
"feasting with silence" - leaves his broth

untouched, sets off with John,
cold pork in pocket, fishes in the lake.
Her Journals sparkle, bring them both to life.
She mends old clothes, spreads linen, hoes the peas,
but never views herself in a true light.
Writer, observer, fitly linked with those
whose pen illuminates - a poet in prose.

* Coleridge's description of Dorothy Wordsworth

George Eliot's Tribute to George Lewes

Saying he owed me his prosperity,
his happiness - husband in all but name -
he cherished me, encouraged, set me free

of self-distrust, distress, helped me to see
that life together could be life aflame.
Saying he owed me his prosperity,

his love and care providing guarantee
of that safe haven needed, I could claim
he cherished me, encouraged, set me free.

In that sweet background of stability
he set my mind alight and brought me fame.
Saying he owed me his prosperity

with head held high, living in love, carefree
despite the world's complaint, I felt no shame.
He cherished me, encouraged, set me free,

became my joy, my all, security
against the slings and arrows that inflame.
Saying he owed me his prosperity,
he cherished me, encouraged, set me free.

Trollope at Waltham

Bordering Essex he found the house
suited him well - first leased then bought it
farmed a little, gardened, listing fruit,
vegetables, a regular
nurseryman's catalogue. And roses,
these for his wife whom he envisaged
dispensing tea under the great cedar.

Stables roomy enough for hunters,
the Essex pack kennelled ten miles off.
Twelve years there the luckiest of his life,
most of his best work achieved
under his own roof. Ambition, hope
come to fruition and all that childhood longing
for affection, friends, swallowed up in joy.

Called at 5.30 by an old groom,
watch set before him, he could write his stint
of three fixed hours spent on articles,
novels before the day's work. Later,
entertaining at home or playing whist
at his Club, he was conscious of success,
fully savoured his present happiness.

'A sweet old prim chill house' - thus Anne Thackeray
visiting in snow. For him full summer
warmed by the sun's ray.

A Clutch of Lad's Love
(Helen Thomas speaks)

My temperament - lighthearted, bright,
inclined to gaiety - his dark moods
threatened me. To enter that black hollow
cautioned.... Yet I longed to go,
to help, to ease. But could not follow.

On those fierce days
of brooding loneliness
I could but mourn my loss.
His cloud of spirit brought
such bitter speech. "Leave me. Get out".

What words to freeze my heart!
I shrivelled in despair,
was paralysed. Black night
then blotted out all love,
all light.
For shouldering off
my plain-seen misery, he'd show
dislike, contempt.... Could see in me
mere cause for self-reproach
and so could say: I hate.

It was not true.
Truer by far to speak
of Love's sweet way.
"No one so much as you".

An Invitation to Tea
(William Bellows accompanies Edmund Gosse
to Max Gate, 29 June 1927)

Setting off, sun shining,
new vistas ahead and the distant moorland
blue, we drew near at last
to 'Casterbridge'; asked the way
to Max Gate....

Turning into a gravel drive,
found the house hidden among bushes.

So this was Hardy at eighty-eight!
Figure erect, hair silvered,
a lined face but the voice youthful.
Welcome waited at table;
there were raspberries - what raspberries!

And such talk! Gosse leading,
myself the stranger offering
a modest, occasional word.
We spoke of D'Urberville tombs
recently seen, the battered stonework.

Vandals, said Hardy: and then all
settled down to story-telling.

No tired author this. Voice well-sustained,
eyes twinkling, a man sprightly
in mind and act. Skipping upstairs
he brought down books,
Tess translated into fine French.

We asked a photograph.
And was our host still writing?
His wife assured us.... Time then to go.
Sun on the road; all still on 'Egdon Heath'.
A day to savour, remember.

For a Poet-Critic

I like him for his honesty, his skill
to fix a pictured scene, invite me in
to share a mood, capture my senses, fill
a need or satisfy some want within.

Poet, historian, critic, just but kind.
To those whose work he reads a generous phrase
meant to encourage every unknown friend.
Where verse deserves, a word of liberal praise.

His language intricate, scholarly, taut
shrewdly evaluated in debate
for the *mot juste* best to perfect his thought,
adjective, adverb to adjust its weight.

The rhythmic Welsh with Anglo-tempered steel
making for structured speech-forms - forceful, real.

Carnival

Near-ninety, he remembers the Clifton
Carnival, far cry from medieval
orgiastic prelude, the common run
to Lent. His was a small boy's annual
August-time festival, a special sweet
long-waited-for, counting-the-days-for, treat.

No ancient Saturnalia - bearpit,
frenetic dance, wineglass filled to the brim,
riotous revelry. Enjoyment of it
began with processional band, for him
the town-trail of a painted caravan,
steam-engine, envying the driver-man.

Came the great day, a tedious drawn-out hour
of queue at the gate, excitement within.
Sound of the shrill steam-organ's thrilling power,
swoosh of Giant Slide, shrieky whistle-din,
stallholders' shouts, clack of coconut shies,
the crowd's loud jeers, triumphant winners' cries.

At last the Roundabout! His chosen horse
head-high, flared nostrils, mane and tail
a twisted rope, races its windblown course
to bring romance, rapture that cannot fail.
Mounting its back, spurring its dappled sides,
soldier-Crusader, knight, he rides, he rides!

Last Journey
(remembering Keith Hart at Telford)

Following the coffin
strapped to the open-topped lorry
we thought of him - a life cut short.

Considering the miles of wide road,
those lapped-up distances
swallowing day, night of his brief life,
we might have expected some great pile-up
jangled carcasses, brakes screaming,
police lights flashing,
ambulances weaving a way
through tangled wreckage.

It was not like that.... Secret cells
started a slow-down,
raced at last with the speed
of a fast lane. Cancer
not accident
had overtaken him.

"More at home in a lorry than a hearse"
he joked, knowing no hope.
So we companioned him
on his old working route,
took our journey to the truck-stop,
mourned his passing, drank tea,
toasted his memory
in a favourite cafe.

Outside, in the rain-wet carpark,
time for reflection.... Who models
the countryside today,
patterns the road, shapes trade?
Men like Keith
driving lorries?

Old Miner

Like an old rock
eroded by tidewash,
the constant knock of time,
he sits half-hid
stolidly obdurate.
Long used to dark
he does not want the sun.

Work underground
from the green age of ten,
pit-scarred, broken by falls,
the past's harshness,
he is well satisfied
with ease, old age,
his present seat in shade.

Out of the mine
the grateful days are kind.
Poor still but pension-proud
he can now smile,
see with unclouded eyes
the cage of life,
his view for fifty years.

Tree Surgeon

A man of stature, strength,
he strides the lawn,
keen, resolute for work.

From my high room
I see him scan the sky -
note outgrowths, mark
each awkward jut
that jars the whole tree-form:
stand back, reflect, create
mind-picture for the frame.

Long pruners trim
low branches - elbow off
stray spars.... He climbs, is lost
to sight but reappears.
Shouldering aside
a tangled limb,
now lets the daylight in
with studied skill.

Down on the ground again
he sorts tools, turns,
sees me and smiles
with quiet confidence.

He means to shape
my future, cheer my spring -
promise such fruit as autumn,
without him, could not bring.

Molecatcher

Despatcher of moles, he walks
a free man under the sky.
Knowing his fell intent you might
not note the pity in his eye.

Day after lonely day
he scans rich earth, distributes death.
Sometimes the noose or trap
fixed in the run;
sometimes the cut and lacerated worm
tipped from a poison can.

Earning his honest bread, he finds
a plover's eager brood –
the skylark resting low in grass –
a hedgehog's spiny ball.
His camera's sympathetic glance
sees and records them all.

Outside his comfortable home
night-lines of corpses are pinned up,
frieze to defy the wind.
Cosy within,
the molecatcher sorts his slides,
rejoices at the natural life therein.

V   REMEMBRANCES

Prep School

I like to think of them,
boys out of school, scattered
over half the known globe.

Start of term, they assemble
a motley collection;
some swept from stranger homes

in a far land; briefly here
to learn, absorb
our alien way of life.

What thoughts on first
arrival? The washed-out skin
of northern climes, cool food,

no spice, the colder glance
outside the warm school walls?
Or is it the amazing green

of English fields broad-spread,
sweet shade of summer trees,
or tender buds in early spring?

For Anniversary 1996

Forty years on - then fifty, sixty, more
and now to seventy-five. What is the power
that keeps in mind and holds a memory green
of times, events that far-off days have seen?

School passes, work-terms come, life follows on.
No time to wonder where the days have gone
until old age gives leisure to detect
the strength that school created, and reflect

that school can root us, give us wings to fly
our farthest reach, perhaps to touch the sky.

Epitaph

It falls folded
from the pile,
a child's school overall
neat, clean, as though
freshly laundered:
Reminds me of Judith in life,
her death an equal lesson in order.
How she would chide -
but gently - each forgetful girl
at start of term, praise those
whose chattels came complete
nothing omitted.

I remember her
brave, patient
to the last, rejecting pity.
Noting the trim stitches
carefully placed, creating pattern
satisfying as existence
well-lived, whole, certain,
I put aside
the scarce-worn smock
for the rummage-sale.
She would have said
there are always other children.

Old Books

Outdated, seldom read, marching
discordantly with more
sophisticated loves on upper shelves,
I cannot part with them. Once
in reformist mood
banished to backroom space,
the blank emptiness
failing to tempt resettlement
stared for a whole day scandalised.

Low, near the floor, those early books
sit humbled, unassuming. Dusty,
the worn spines faded now by light
long gone, suns filtering
through trim dawn curtains,
blazing at noon, slanted
at evensong on Sundays lost
in a past limbo of jaded time, they still
have power to hold. Not altogether
tarnished, the gold
threads childhood's track, leads
through a tortuous adolescent maze
to present questioning. With these
old trusted friends of half-forgotten days
I am enamoured still. Have they become
inherent part of me? How do we thrive,
progress? As we best can,
lives carved by what we find,
child prompting, fathering the full-grown man.

Grandfather Clock

Facing me squarely whenever
I come into the room
it meets me jubilant
speaks of long survival.
Has counted already the hours
of full two hundred years
implies my days are carefully numbered.

Greeting me later
with grave obsequiousness
as I climb the stair
to that daily death in life
Shakespeare calls sleep,
it reminds me time and again
of its own timelessness.
My minutes tick
are gone. Whispering
"you have not time to lose,
little to spare", the clock
time out of mind ticks on.

Time enough, I reply.
No mere observer, I
can feel, act out
in free-will incident life's art.
Your dull monotonous mechanics, clock
work only when I play my part.

Shipwreck

Two years later I still dream of it,
wake in a wash of sweat. The ravening wave
tips and topples the ship, rears up a helpless toy,
swallows the sky in an easy mouthful.

Swept from the submerged rim, I am lightly tossed
flotsam on a frantic yeasty surface.
Limbs hopelessly flailing flinch on impact
of ice-bite in the sea's thick-curdled glass.

Drowned by a huge obliterating wall,
my choked cry gropes for sound in the nightmare room.
A rope thrown out, blown free by jubilant gale
rips in fifty-knot winds long trails of foam.

Poor human sack hauled through the grey crouched wave,
salvaged on deck I gulp in noisy spurts,
fear for the lost, cower in my frozen self,
strain for the flap of the helicopter's whirr.

Emptied by grief, winched up, I watch the boat
drift on her lonely path. At this the dream
dissolves in a waking blur. In a sweat
of transient fear I search for the steady wall,

the window's open eye. Grasp at the gift
of a new day's cloudless, reassuring sky.

Passport to Ecstasy

First engine failing and seeing
a strange luminous glow, the crew
feared turbulence - told us quickly
to fasten seatbelts. Grey smoke spread,
thickened. Someone called out
that flame danced on a wing.

A woman fainted.... Through blue haze
black cloud billowed. Appalled
as white light turned pink, then orange,
we heard a grating sound. Two more
engines exploded, set the crew
in flurries of action.... Too stunned

to move, no one panicked. But knees
trembling as jelly, hands shaking,
I quietly cried. And as the last
engine's death-throe faded, there came
a jolt of silence. Two stewards touched.
A goodbye token? Yet the crew

still laboured.... I thought of friends, possessions,
all that was dear and jibbed
at threat of death - in split seconds
reviewed my life, too precious now
to lose. Swift rushes of anger
stressed the waste, complete helplessness.

Utter despair overcame.... Then,
incredibly, engines roared,
another leapt to action. Disbelief
melted in a flood of tears,
all desperate thought, lonely grief drowned
in that honeyed miracle of sound.

Anna at Four

Offering a hand of trust to all, she tests
response; learns, grows, accepts all that is found
in an old world full of guile. Today, rests
innocent of tripwires hidden around.
Colour and form of bird, flower, butterfly -
this huge expanding globe seems to unravel
countless surprises, all to multiply
her wide-eyed joy in the long day's travel.

Seeing life free of threat, no forest dark
with secret menace, what of tomorrow?
She cannot know her ship must soon embark
on seas that flood these troubled shores with sorrow.
Just now, ecstatic eyes observe, content,
and tiny fingers probe, experiment.

For Helen

Your card comes, midsummer token
of a distant link (double generation gap)
tenuous, flimsy, but as yet unbroken.
A morning sun throws brightness on the scene.
Shadows are minimal and, towering
above, your castle rooted in the air
proclaims hopes fixed and firmly centred there.
Weather, the villa, everything
(your message says) is fine. You'll write sometime,
but now the day's too full for anything.

Dear girl of eighteen summers, if you knew
how swift years flow, how crowded hours become
your hope, but slender now, would grow still less.
So let's cry quits. No idle promises.

Mother and Son
(The Autistic)

Such hope I had! But where the child
I looked for in those joyous months
of buoyant confidence - the son
I longed for to complete our love?

I cannot reach him: trapped, remote
in some dark dream, he cries all night,
seeming so terrified. His eyes
search vaguely, move uneasily.

Hostile, disturbed, he closely clings
to the small toy I gave to soothe
a fretful hour. How should so poor
a thing, inanimate, please more

than mothercare? I weep but this
brings no response.... The passing months,
slow years confirm his ritual
obsessions, never bring release.

Imprisoned in distress, encased
each in a coiled and twisted shell,
we drown half-lost in enmity.
Yet how can there exist such pain

Mother to son, both seeking love?
My ceaseless probe to find a way
into his mind and heart, unlock
his prison door, sometimes reveals

a fitful glimpse of him. And then
what momentary gain.... Too soon
blank walls close in to leave more loss
wrapped in my insecurity.

Memory, Hold the Door

We cannot catch the years as they fly past.
They should be netted, trapped-in-amber flies
set in a seal of gold - a treasured prize
of age, not sunk in the mind's pool, or cast
into some limbo of forgotten time.

Each several hour becomes a jewel when
the day gives leisure to look back, to try
to capture grief or a lost ecstasy.
These make our sum of life, and it is then
we long to resurrect rhythm and rhyme

of a tale now rounding to its destined
end. Nearing completion, the necklace needs
every component part, its fill of beads.
In that horrific crisis, were we sinned
against or sinning? Why no thought to climb

down from our pedestal to meet the claim
of others on that day they cried for aid?
And of those spells of joy, when all was laid
before us, our whole world lit with flame,
why can we glean such thin grain from our prime?

No answer comes. Time's passage was too fleet
and all is dark. The story's incomplete.

To an Eighty-year Old

Through your eyes
I see old aunts,
a whole family,
retrospect festivals
and the great Christmas gathering of clans.
Your thumbnail sketches
idiosyncratic, vivid
convey a child's lively views
developed in man's allotted span.

Through your eyes
I see a world
that was never mine
defined, epitomised,
bearing taste of lost tradition:
Victorian jewels
attractive Edwardian gems
borne in a small boy's bright mind
facets time-polished to shine anew.

Through your eyes
I catch glimpses
of an oasis
of peace, security
preceding today's dissident turmoil.
With ripe acumen
you bring wit, judicial wisdom
to a crazy universe,
clarity to a perplexed jungle.

Through your eyes
I share a past,
forget present,
see golden possibility
of a better future.

Doors

Wishing to print me
plainly into his past life,
he took me places,
opened doors on his old world –
put me right in the picture
of all his loves.

This was existence
beyond my narrow sphere –
a framework of family
warm, close, in roomy houses
with scope for growth:
youth with promise of more.
Doors opening
on flowers, fields,
a rare seashore.

From my prison
of early limits,
doors that had walled me in,
he led me out,
made me feel free.
Slowly became my world,
wholly encompassed me.

Redress

Seeing his need
I stitched for him, made shirts,
a dressing-gown - clothed him with love
instead of enmity.
How could she thus despise
a man so pliant, generous?
There had been more than disregard
of outward care - a scorn
of all he tried to do -
his work, philosophy.

Inner resentment grew,
tore him apart. This too
I saw although no words were said.
Seams of his life split through
I tried to mend - could only bind,
patch up. And this I gladly did
but knew repairs were tenuous.
Beneath the superficial smooth
the rough remained.... And yet
somehow, in some strange way,
for both of us
this substance was enough.

X-ray

Stripped of delusion covering fear with hope,
we are excoriate by this machine.
Here all pretensions leave; the hidden truth
reveals itself upon the open screen.
This eye, pervasive and percipient
probes through the flesh that clothes the secret worm,
flashes the false intrusion into view,
detects each deviation from the norm.
　　No argument: the inquisition ray,
impartial and impervious to age
or wealth illuminates the tell-tale script
emergent on the frankly-mirrored page.
Evasion serves no more: enlightened, we
must meet the nescient dark unflinchingly.

The Threat

The certain day
unmarked as yet
in any calendar
draws daily nearer -
casts its dark shadow
on every glimpse of sun.

Thought of the hidden growth
secretly eating
pursues me. Love
that seemed so strong
to ward off ill,
protect, indemnify,

has lost its power.
Mocking at hope,
helplessly groping,
shrivels attempts
to keep at bay
the looming cloud.

Insidiously
death creeps upon the scene.
Keeping my tenuous grip
on cheerfulness,
I try to smile,
let fly some cut-and-thrust

of feeble joke.
You parry, turn the blade
and take my hand.
Courage is all,
you seem to say. I nod
as if I understand.

Grief

No sleep - sleep had become
a fitful luxury
in those last months: the sum
of ease but two or three
brief hours of pillow-rest
in a blank apathy.

Dawn that October day
crept slow, insidiously,
filtering ray by ray
into my room. Misty
late morning, a grey sky
lightening reluctantly.

Heavy, loaded with care
I rose laboriously,
weighed down by grief, aware
that this must go with me
throughout the long-drawn span
of Time this hour began.

No food. I set it out
for guests. But he not there
(he who had shared throughout)
I had no will to share.
My dearest guest away,
could find no words to say

to friends who talked of a man
they knew, but did not love
as I had loved. I ran
to none for comfort, strove
to hide my deeper grief,
sorrow beyond relief.

Days raced with him: no strings
could hold the flying hour.
Successive years grew wings,
unfolding as a flower
opens to the swift sun,
closes when day is done.

In church they sang his hymn.
I could not sing, for tears
choked at my throat for him.
Through all those happy years
I sang with joy - but then
I could not mourn with them.

At home, alone, no ray
of future hope, for dead
do not return. My way
a road looming ahead,
dark, overcast, to lead
into each coming strung-out day.

Obit

Today he lies
'cribbed, cabined and confined' -
he who but yesterday
moved through the living hours
among his treasured flowers.

Tomorrow will be gone,
a 'handful of grey ash'.
Is life so weak, so frail,
a passing streak,
a summer-lightning flash?

Anniversary

My late rose spills –
but other flowers are brought
to hold you dear. Some are
red cyclamen,
intense as was my grief;
some, yellow sprays
that spread the sun of life
you lit around.

The date brings memories
of harsh traumatic hours
before the sick shocked day
you slipped apart –
the cry for flowers
to deck your room,
my hurried run
for roses potent, live,
to stem the tide of death.

It flows here still.
The autumn flowers bring back
a threat of wintry chill.
And yet I know
your earlier joy
– and mine – has power
to nullify the pain,
make me alive again.

VI BEYOND THE DARK

Elegy

It is the sense of emptiness that grieves.

Without you, days once full of fun,
activity in garden, house
vacantly pall. Being alone,

reading that pleased falls on deaf ears,
the music gone. Past unity
now but a dream, each soundless room,

left without voice of harmony
that gave it life, is a dark shell,
hollow as caves when the tide's gone –

a no-man's land robbed of its sun.
It is the sense of emptiness that grieves.
Yet Christmas roses bud beneath wet leaves.

New Year

It will not bring you back. My diary
now full of empty days that lie ahead,
will not be filled with interest that we
once took joint pleasure in. No - for the dead
do not return: cannot in this world share
with us the daily crosses or the joy
of each day's happiness. Now I must wear
alone the cloak of bliss, the day's annoy.

It cannot bring you back. Yet every page
will hold in memory some rich array
of life together, each new day engage
some recollection of your words, your way.
So shall I meet the coming year with praise,
knowing a part of you is here always.

Light in our Darkness

Eyes clouded by cataract, every tree
climbs unseen skies. Houses rise mountain-high.
Cars, lorries loom bulky as ships at sea,
town traffic lumbers elephantine by.

The road runs nowhere - books are near-closed doors.
Friends greet me lost in mist. I am alone
in a dense world of sound. Feet feel for floors,
stumble up steps. I travel on my own.

I seek my needle out but, focussing,
the thread evades.... But when precision's skill
shall flake the shell, the surgeon's implant bring
new light to eyes that hide their power still,

then trees will put on leaf, flowers shine through rain.
The dark days done, summer will bloom again.

Sky at Night

The huge museum
of night sky
displaying stars, white dwarfs
shrunk suns engulfed
in an unmeasured space
comets and spinning nebulae
holds us entranced.

Merely to contemplate
those great immensities
offers relief from the long
littleness of life.

Pondering origins,
finger of God first moving
in time-frame,
or purpose in the pull
of satellite attraction;
our constant passion
and endless quest.

The Dark and the Light

Each day, each year repeats
a cycle, dark to bright.
Heaven, mutinous with cloud
cracks with a flash of light.

White snowdrops spring
to break the black of earth.
The painter knows that shade
like shine, gives worth.
Flame soars from furnace gloom;
we come from womb to birth.

Dark, light – creative strands
form warp and weft
of the whole scarf of life.
We ask, with bated breath,
what of the light
beyond the dark of Death?

Phoenix at the Abbey
(14.12.1990)

Light washed the rose-hued stone to white:
dark soared to jewelled window-glint -
and far below
a feast of colour, candle-lit.

In slow procession to the choir
turquoise and ruby framed in black
moved, singing, past
casements that caught a fitful fire.

Easy to paint a scene - but how
pin words on music, purest sound
rising to height
beyond all reach, all human flow

of prose or poetry? And where
to seek out phrase and clause to fit
the Dark and Light
of Then and Now - our living share

of earth-born harvest, age to age
written on History's fleeting page?

The Spirit of Man

Even as the candle spends its provident light
After the fading of the sunlit day,
Lifting the darkness from the sombre night,
So does Man's life in service waste away.

In this poor candle is his spirit shrined.
Yet, in its poverty, implicit wealth,
The gold of living sacrifice we find,
In its utility a saving health.

    Divinity in human form is found
    Expressed in heavenly tolerance and love,
    Thus are we to each other surely bound
    Deriving inspiration from above.

And so we to the world a light afford,
The Spirit of Man, the Candle of the Lord.

Indecision

Wavering between the profit and the loss
am apt to find myself continually
trying to pan away the gold from dross.

Now, from this present height, I look across
the gap from age to youth, a farflung sea.
Wavering between the profit and the loss

of a long life, so often put a gloss
on acts that cannot bear it easily.
Trying to pan away the gold from dross

how separate the solid, real from floss
that, evanescent, floats continually?
Wavering between the profit and the loss

I find a tendency to add, emboss,
reluctance to admit adversity.
Trying to pan away the gold from dross

I want to cast away the albatross
of failure, debt, see wealth not poverty.
Wavering between the profit and the loss
how can I pan away the gold from dross?

T.S. Eliot, *Ash Wednesday*:
'Wavering between the profit and the loss'.

Prayer

Because I stand too long
before the mirror of my self-conceit;
because I turn aside
from many whom I meet -
Dear Lord, forgive.

Because I am too blind
to see the sorrow that is all around;
because I am too deaf
to hear all distant sound -
Dear Lord, forgive.

Because too often I
so gladly pass by on the other side;
and fail to hear the cry
of need from far and wide -
Dear Lord, forgive.

Because I fail to do
the good that in my wisdom I have planned;
because I still hold back
my friendly helping hand -
Dear Lord, forgive.

Because I think of him
who might be friend always as enemy;
because I do not say
the words to set him free -
Dear Lord, forgive.

Because my mind is set
too frequently on strife and argument;
because I often let
my heart refuse consent -
Dear Lord, forgive.

Because I have not used
those talents you have given so generously,
but idled time away
in light frivolity -
Dear Lord, forgive.

Dear Lord, forgive my human weaknesses,
my pride, my failures, sin;
exclude me not from Grace
but, of your bounty, let me in.